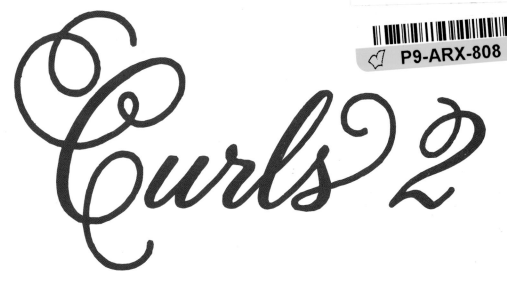

Curls 2

VERSATILE, WEARABLE

WRAPS TO KNIT AT ANY GAUGE

Hunter Hammersen

PANTSVILLE
P R E S S

Charts created with StitchMastery Knitting Chart Editor.

ISBN: 978-0-9849982-7-2

First Printing, 2016

Printed in China

Pantsville Press

Cleveland, Ohio

www.pantsvillepress.com

Contents

Introduction. 1

Anatomy of a Curl. 3

Hints. 6

Gauge, Needles, & Sizing. 7

Charts. 8

Blocking. 9

Patterns

    Mendacity. 10

    Falsity. 14

    Prevarication. 18

    Deceit. 22

    Perfidy. 26

    Pretense. 30

    Taradiddle. 34

    Equivocation. 38

    Artifice. 42

    Cozenage. 46

    Subterfuge. 50

    Trickery. 54

    Chicanery. 58

    Fakery. 62

Thanks. 66

Sources. 67

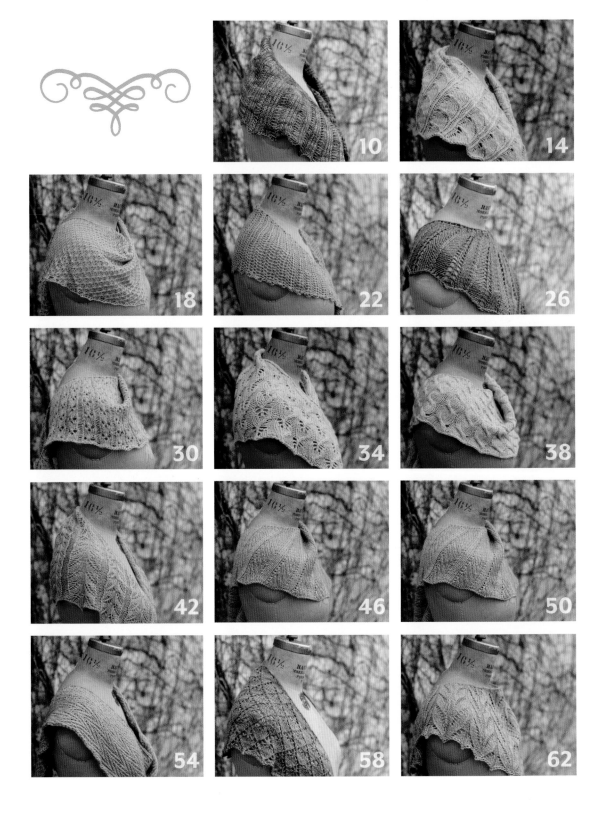

Introduction

Swatches will get you in trouble. Swatches are where this whole thing began, and look where we are now!

It all started innocently enough. I found myself taken with a pretty little stitch pattern and wondered how I might work in some increases while still maintaining the overall pattern. So I started swatching. A little while later, I had a rather interesting shape. I was intrigued, so I kept swatching. A little later still, I had a stack of swatches, pages of scribbled charts, and an idea. That stack of swatches turned into the first Curls book, and now, it's turned into another!

I call the pieces in these books Curls because of their marvelous shape. They're gently curved on both the top and the bottom, which means they drape beautifully around your neck and shoulders (take a look at the picture on the next page if you want to see what they look like laid out flat). It also means that you can knit them small and wear them like a cowl or keep going and end up with a much larger piece to wear like a scarf or a shawl. Perhaps most exciting of all, because the shape is so easy to work with, you can knit them at any gauge, with any weight of yarn, and to any size. They really are just about the most accommodating pieces of knitting you can imagine.

I wanted the projects in this book to show just how flexible Curls really are. The pieces here are worked in everything from a delicate lace-weight to a sturdy worsted-weight. The wingspans range from 40 inches (which is just perfect to tuck under the collar of your jacket) to a whopping 80 inches (which will wrap around your neck twice with length to spare). The quickest took only 300 yards of yarn, while the most ambitious clocked in at 700. But the marvelous thing is that *any* of these patterns would work in *any* of the weights of yarn and look beautiful at *any* of the sizes.

And, just as you can knit your Curl however you like, you can wear it however you like, too. Crumple it up a bit and just toss it around your neck (like Subterfuge, page 50). Fold it in half and pass the ends through the fold like a scarf (like Prevarication, page 18). Throw one end over your shoulder while the other drapes down your chest (like Chicanery, page 15). Tuck the skinny end around the thicker end (like Equivocation, page 41). Form it into a loop and wrap it around your neck (like Mendacity, page 13). Or let the bulk of the piece sit on your chest and bring the ends behind your neck (like Cozenage, page 49). You can't mess it up; I swear I've never found any shape that's so easy to wear.

So grab your favorite skein of yarn and get started. You're in charge, and I know you're going to love the result!

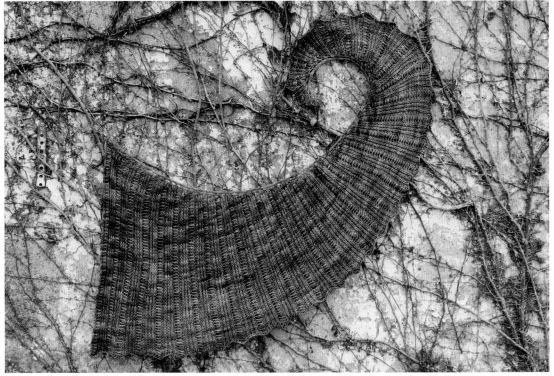

Anatomy of a Curl

Before we dive in, let me say you can totally skip this part (though I do recommend you at least read the Hints section on page 6). It is officially allowed. You can turn to the patterns and dive right in, and everything will come out fine. That's half the fun of these projects. They just sort of work on their own! I will never know you skipped ahead, and your Curls will be lovely.

But if you do want to understand what's going on (either to modify the patterns provided here or to make up your own), this is the place to be.

I'll begin by taking you through the pieces of a Curl. Then I'll talk a bit about how a Curl comes together, how the charts are laid out, and some of the modifications you might see from one pattern to the next.

This diagram shows the five pieces of a Curl.

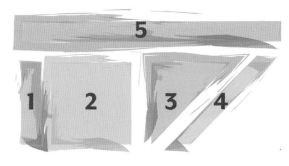

The pictures on the facing page show two Curls, Perfidy (top) and Mendacity (bottom), spread out flat and oriented more or less the way you'd wear them. The bound off edge (section 5) is on the bottom. The increases (section 4) are on the top. The edge (section 1) is on the left or right.

1 **EDGE** This section makes up the straight edge on one side of the Curl. It will be two or more stitches wide and will have as many rows as the main repeat.

2 **MAIN REPEAT** This section is the main attraction. It's the pattern that makes up the field of your Curl. It can be any size.

3 **WEDGE** This section prepares you for the next instance of the main repeat. Its size and shape are the most variable of all the pieces. It will have as many rows as the main repeat, and its width will be a multiple of the width of the main repeat. It will often incorporate parts of the stitch pattern found in the main repeat.

4 **INCREASES** This section lets your Curl grow. It gives you the new stitches the wedge needs. It will be four to six stitches wide (and the stitch count may vary from row to row) and will be as tall as the main repeat.

5 **FINISH** This gets your stitches ready to bind off. Sometimes it's one row, sometimes it's several, and sometimes it's not there at all.

These five pieces, taken together, make up the most basic Curl. But if you just knit that, you'd have a tiny piece of fabric. The magic happens when you continue to repeat the edge, main repeat, wedge, and increases. Each time you repeat them, your knitting gets bigger, and it starts to form a lovely curved shape.

It all works because the wedge and the increases make room for more copies of the main repeat. That means that once you've worked through your edge, main repeat, wedge, and increases once, you've got the right number of stitches to work through them again, this time with one (or more) extra repeats of the main repeat.

This is so much easier to see with a diagram. This picture shows a series of edge, main repeat, wedge, and increases worked four times. See how the number of the main repeat increases? That's how your Curl grows.

Now to keep the charts to a reasonable size (and to prevent them from looking too daunting), they'll look more like the diagram on the previous page than like the one below. That is, they'll generally only show you one set of edge, main repeat, wedge, and increases sections (plus the finish if you need it). You'll just keep working the main repeat as needed until the Curl is the size you want. And don't worry, the colors on the charts match up with what you're seeing here, and there's always a note with all the numbers you might need. Once you've got the stitches on your needles, I think you'll find the whole process very intuitive!

Part of the fun of Curls is their flexibility. While the principles outlined above hold for all Curls, there are lots of variations. I'd like to outline a few here just so you're not surprised when you come across them in the patterns.

Each individual pattern will have a little guide like the ones shown on the next page that maps out the shape and growth of that particular Curl.

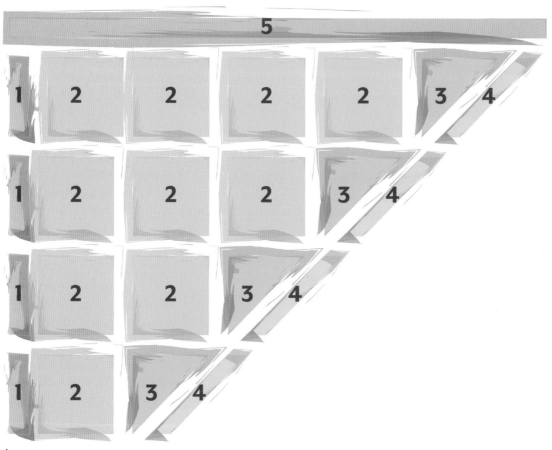

FLIP THINGS AROUND There's no reason the edge has to be on the left. It works just as well on the right. About half the patterns have the edge on the left and half on the right.

START WITH A WEDGE Often, especially if the main repeat is rather wide, there's not a good way to jump in with a main repeat right from the start. In those cases, you can start with a wedge and use it to create the space you need a little farther into the piece.

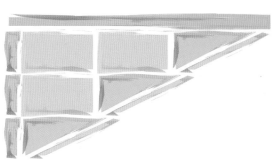

LEAVE SOME PIECES OUT Sometimes you don't need a special chart to be ready to bind off, and the pattern may not include a finish section.

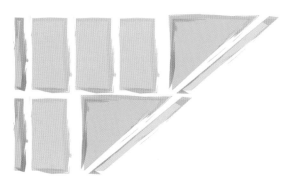

CHANGE THE SLOPE In the example we started with, there was room for one more main repeat every time you worked through the series of edge, main repeat, wedge, and increases. But that isn't set in stone. You can make space for two or three or even more extra main repeats each time. It all depends on how fast the Curl grows. Different rates of increase will give you different finished proportions.

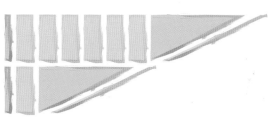

Hints

BLOCKING See page 9.

CAST ON These cast ons are quite short, so you can use whatever cast on you like best. The projects here use the long-tailed cast on.

CAST OFF The bound-off edge needs to be very stretchy, I recommend Jeny's Surprisingly Stretchy Bind Off as seen in the Fall 2009 issue of *Knitty*. You're welcome to use another, but it is important to make sure it's stretchy!

CHARTS See page 8.

GAUGE See page 7.

NEEDLES See page 7.

RIGHT-SIDE ROW Right-side rows are worked with the public side of the Curl facing you. While you knit them, read the chart from right to left and follow the right-side notations in the stitch key. See page 8 for more.

SIZING See page 7.

SLIPPED STITCHES All of the projects call for slipping stitches along the edge of the knitting to create a tidy selvage edge. There are almost as many ways to do this as there are knitters. If you're getting elongated stitches along the edge of the fabric, you're doing it right!

One approach that works for most people is to always slip the first stitch as if to purl with your yarn held to the wrong side of the fabric. If you find that's not working for the way you knit, you can also try holding the yarn to the back of the work and slipping as if to knit on right-side rows and holding the yarn to the front of the work and slipping as if to purl on wrong-side rows.

STITCH DEFINITIONS Any unusual or potentially unknown stitches are defined as you encounter them. Look for the grey boxes with each pattern for the details of that pattern's fancy stitchwork.

STITCH MARKERS You may find it helpful to separate each instance of the main repeat with a stitch marker.

SWATCHES Swatches are always a good idea. Always. That said, these projects are unusually forgiving, and getting a particular gauge isn't important (as long as you like the fabric you're getting, see page 7 for more about this). If you wanted to just start knitting and judge your fabric once you're a few inches in, I won't tell.

WINGSPAN This is the edge created by the stitches you add when you work the increases. It is opposite the bound-off edge and will likely be closest to your neck when you wear your Curl.

WRONG-SIDE ROW Wrong-side rows are worked with the private side of the Curl facing you. While you knit them, read the chart from left to right and follow the wrong-side notations in the stitch key. See page 8 for more.

YARN REQUIREMENTS Each pattern lists a generous estimate for the yarn needed to complete the project *as shown in the picture*. This is a good guideline, but estimating yardage requirements is a bit of a black art. If you decide to make your Curl with a different weight of yarn or in a different finished size, you'll need a different amount of yarn. See page 7 for more about this. Luckily, these are perfect knit-until-the-yarn-runs-out projects!

Gauge, Needles, & Sizing

One of the most marvelous things about Curls is their flexibility. You can use just about any weight of yarn, and you can make them in whatever size you'd like. That's wonderful, and it gives you a tremendous amount of freedom to create exactly what you want, but it does mean I can't tell you too much about your gauge, which needles to use, how big to make your Curl, or how much yarn you'll need.

Think about it for a moment. If I show you a Curl worn as a cowl and made with fingering-weight yarn, and you decide to knit that same Curl to wear as a shawl using a worsted-weight yarn, of course you're going to get a different gauge, use different needles, end up with a different size, and use a different number of yards of yarn. That's how it's *supposed* to work. These patterns give you the freedom to use whatever yarn you choose and to make whatever size you'd like.

I've listed the gauge for the samples shown in the book, but you don't need to worry about matching it. The most important thing to remember about gauge is that *if you're getting a fabric you like, you've got the right gauge!* If, as you work, you find you want a tighter, firmer fabric, go down a needle size. If you want a looser, drapier fabric, go up a needle size. You're in complete control.

The same applies for the size of your Curl. Have a small skein of yarn? Make a cowl. The smallest project shown here used just under 300 yards of yarn. And if you want to make a giant shawl to snuggle up in, you can do that too. You're in charge. If you're happy, it's perfect.

I do recommend checking the size of your Curl from time to time as they have been known to grow rather quickly. To do that, you're going to want to stretch it out to its full size. The edge with the live stitches wants to curve, so you need to get your stitches onto something flexible. If you're using circulars and your cable is long enough, you can use that (being careful not to let stitches pop off the ends). If not, a piece of waste yarn will do the trick. Just transfer your stitches to a piece of waste yarn, spread your Curl out flat, and see if you've got the size you like (go ahead and give it a good tug as most knitting grows a bit with blocking).

Charts

I love charts. They're a great way to present a large amount of information in a small amount of space. But as much as I love them, I realize that they can seem a bit daunting if you're not used to them. Once you get to know them though, they're really not hard. The most important thing to remember is that charts show you a stylized picture of the right side of your work. Keep that in mind, and you're halfway there!

The easiest way to get to know a chart is to work through an example. So let's talk through this sample chart step by step.

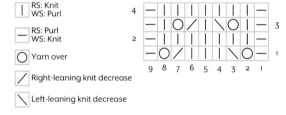

Always start with row 1, which is always the bottom row. First, figure out if row 1 is a right-side row or a wrong-side row. The instructions will tell you, but you can also tell from the chart. If it's a right-side row, the row number will be on the right of the chart. If it's a wrong-side row, the row number will be on the left of the chart.

In this example, row 1 is a right-side row.

Now start knitting! Just read across the chart and make the stitches in the order they're shown. Since you're working a right-side row, you'll work across the row from right to left and make the stitches as indicated by the right-side (RS) entries in the stitch key.

Row 1: purl 1, yarn over, work a left-leaning knit decrease, knit 3, work a right-leaning knit decrease, yarn over, purl 1.

Next, move on to row 2. All the patterns in this book are worked flat, so you'll always turn your work at the end of every row. Row 2 is a wrong-side row. Since you're working a wrong-side row, you'll work across the chart from left to right and make the stitches as indicated by the wrong-side (WS) entries in the stitch key. If a stitch doesn't have both RS and WS entries, it's either only worked on right-side rows, or it's the same on both right-side and wrong-side rows.

Row 2: knit 1, purl 7, knit 1.

Turn your work again, and move on to row 3, a right-side row.

Row 3: purl 1, knit 1, yarn over, work a left-leaning knit decrease, knit 1, work a right-leaning knit decrease, yarn over, knit 1, purl 1.

Turn your work again and move to row 4, a wrong-side row.

Row 4: knit 1, purl 7, and knit 1.

That's really all there is to it! Some charts are bigger, but the basic principles always hold.

The only other thing you might want to pay attention to is stitch repeats. These are indicated by heavy borders surrounding blocks of stitches. When you see these, you know you'll need to repeat the stitches within the borders as described in the stitch key and notes. You may want to separate stitch repeats with stitch markers to help you keep track of them.

Blocking

Curls pop into shape with blocking. The pieces here have all been vigorously blocked, and you'll almost certainly want to do the same with yours.

Start by soaking your Curl in cool water for at least half an hour. Then, roll it up in a towel and gently squeeze out the excess water.

Unroll it, lay it out on your blocking surface (I use blocking mats, but a bed or even a clean carpet will work), and pat it into shape.

Your shape will look something like the swatches below or the pictures on page 2 though the precise shape will change depending on which pattern you're following.

You can block your Curl with pins or with a combination of pins and blocking wires. If you're using only pins, pin out the straight edge first (I use a ruler to keep it nice and even). Next, stretch the top edge (that's your bound-off edge) and pin it in place. If you're using pins and blocking wires, start by threading your wires through the bound-off edge (I like to look for landmarks in the pattern repeat, for example a cable cross or a decrease, and always go through the same spot), then pin out the straight edge, and finally pin out the wires. In either case, be sure to use rust-proof pins.

Go ahead and give your work a good, firm tug as you're blocking to really open up your stitches. Depending on the pattern, the edge may have ripples or be smooth. You can emphasize any ripples by where you put your pins or run your wire.

Finally, let it dry completely (I know it's hard, but it's important) before carefully unpinning.

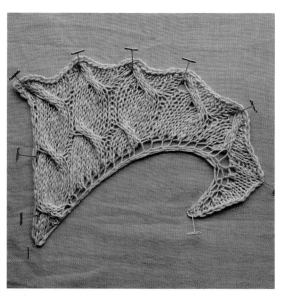

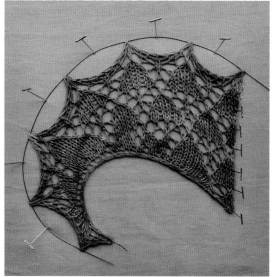

Mendacity

SHOWN IN Rastita, a DK-weight yarn by Malabrigo, in the color Plomo.

GAUGE & SIZING Shown at 26 stitches in 4 inches in pattern as charted. The piece shown used 475 yards of yarn and has a wingspan of 40 inches.

CAST ON Cast on 11 stitches.

BODY Odd rows are wrong-side rows. Even rows are right-side rows.

Work the Chart, repeating the 4 rows surrounded by the thick border as described in the key and note, until Curl reaches desired size. Each wrong-side row increases the stitch count by 2. Each right-side row increases the stitch count by 3. Stop after completing row 8 of the Chart.

Work the Finish Chart once. You'll repeat the 10 stitches surrounded by the purple border as needed to use up your stitches.

FINISHING Bind off loosely using a stretchy bind off. Weave in ends. Block to shape.

Shape

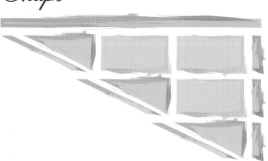

Chart

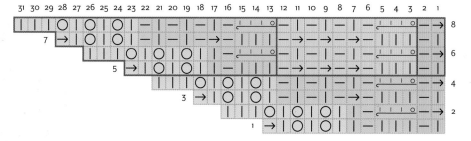

Finish Chart

RS: Knit
WS: Purl

RS: Purl
WS: Knit

Slip as if to purl

Yarn over

Yarn over cluster

Repeat these 4 rows until Curl reaches desired size. With each new repeat, work the yellow stitches 1 more time.

Repeat these 10 stitches as needed.

NOTE The 4 rows surrounded by the thick border are repeated to adjust the size of the Curl. The first time you work them, work the block of yellow stitches once. The second time you work them, work the block of yellow stitches 2 times. Each subsequent time you work them, work the block of yellow stitches 1 more time.

YARN OVER CLUSTER Yarn over, knit 3, pass the yarn over over those 3 stitches and off the needle.

Falsity

SHOWN IN Devon, a DK-weight yarn by Black Bunny Fibers, in the color Cloudfall.

GAUGE & SIZING Shown at 20 stitches in 4 inches in pattern as charted. The piece shown used 450 yards of yarn and has a wingspan of 44 inches.

CAST ON Cast on 10 stitches.

BODY Odd rows are wrong-side rows. Even rows are right-side rows.

Work the Chart, repeating the 8 rows surrounded by the thick border as described in the key and note, until Curl reaches desired size. Each wrong-side row increases the stitch count by 1. Each right-side row increases the stitch count by 2. Stop after completing row 16 of the Chart.

Work the Finish Chart once. You'll repeat the 12 stitches surrounded by the purple border as needed to use up your stitches.

FINISHING Bind off loosely using a stretchy bind off. Weave in ends. Block to shape.

NOTE The 8 rows surrounded by the thick border are repeated to adjust the size of the Curl. The first time you work them, work the block of yellow stitches once. The second time you work them, work the block of yellow stitches 2 times. Each subsequent time you work them, work the block of yellow stitches 1 more time.

LEFT-LEANING TWISTED KNIT DECREASE Insert the right needle from the right to the left into the back loops of 2 stitches. Knit them both together.

LEFT-LEANING TWISTED PURL DECREASE Purl 2 together through the back loops.

Shape

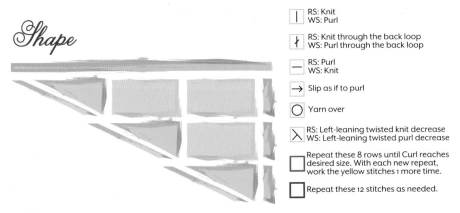

	RS: Knit WS: Purl
	RS: Knit through the back loop WS: Purl through the back loop
	RS: Purl WS: Knit
	Slip as if to purl
	Yarn over
	RS: Left-leaning twisted knit decrease WS: Left-leaning twisted purl decrease
	Repeat these 8 rows until Curl reaches desired size. With each new repeat, work the yellow stitches 1 more time.
	Repeat these 12 stitches as needed.

Chart

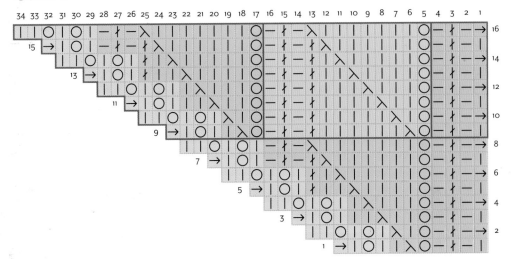

Finish Chart

Prevarication

SHOWN IN Shangri La, a lace-weight yarn by Bijou Basin Ranch, in the color Silver.

GAUGE & SIZING Shown at 20 stitches in 4 inches in pattern as charted. The piece shown used 550 yards of yarn and has a wingspan of 46 inches.

CAST ON Cast on 8 stitches.

BODY Odd rows are wrong-side rows. Even rows are right-side rows.

Work the Chart, repeating the 4 rows surrounded by the thick border as described in the key and note, until Curl reaches desired size. Each row increases the stitch count by 2. Stop after completing row 8 of the Chart.

Work a final row by slipping the first stitch as if to purl and purling to the end.

FINISHING Bind off loosely using a stretchy bind off. Weave in ends. Block to shape.

Shape

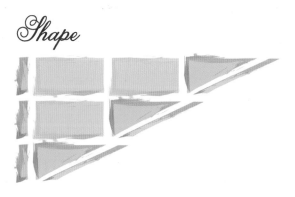

Chart

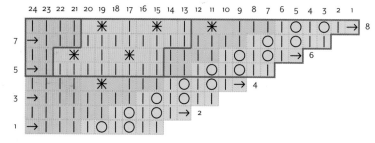

NOTE The 4 rows surrounded by the thick border are repeated to adjust the size of the Curl. The first time you work them, work the block of yellow stitches once. The second time you work them, work the block of yellow stitches 2 times. Each subsequent time you work them, work the block of yellow stitches 1 more time.

THREE STITCH CLUSTER Knit 3 together but do not take the stitches off the needle, yarn over, knit 3 together again and do take the stitches off the needle.

Deceit

SHOWN IN Serena, a sport-weight yarn by Manos del Uruguay, in the color Seal.

GAUGE & SIZING Shown at 24 stitches in 4 inches in pattern as charted. The piece shown used 300 yards of yarn and has a wingspan of 50 inches.

CAST ON Cast on 8 stitches.

BODY Odd rows are right-side rows. Even rows are wrong-side rows.

Work the Chart, repeating the 8 rows surrounded by the thick border as described in the key and note, until Curl reaches desired size. Each right-side row increases the stitch count by 1. Each wrong-side row increases the stitch count by 2. Stop after completing row 16 of the Chart.

Work a final row by slipping the first stitch as if to purl and knitting to the end.

FINISHING Bind off loosely using a stretchy bind off. Weave in ends. Block to shape.

Shape

Chart

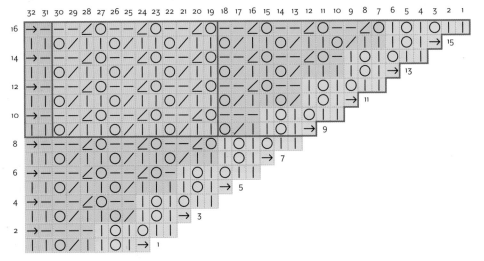

	RS: Knit WS: Purl
—	WS: Knit (this symbol only appears on wrong-side rows)
→	Slip as if to purl
O	Yarn over
/	Right-leaning knit decrease
∠	WS: Right-leaning knit decrease (this symbol only appears on the wrong-side rows)
☐	Repeat these 8 rows until Curl reaches desired size. With each new repeat, work the yellow stitches 3 more times.

NOTE The 8 rows surrounded by the thick border are repeated to adjust the size of the Curl. The first time you work them, work the block of yellow stitches once. The second time you work them, work the block of yellow stitches 2 times. Each subsequent time you work them, work the block of yellow stitches 1 more time.

RIGHT-LEANING KNIT DECREASE Knit 2 together.

Perfidy

SHOWN IN Sweater, a worsted-weight yarn by Spud & Chloë, in the color 7525.

GAUGE & SIZING Shown at 16 stitches in 4 inches in pattern as charted. The piece shown used 450 yards of yarn and has a wingspan of 50 inches.

CAST ON Cast on 8 stitches.

BODY Odd rows are wrong-side rows. Even rows are right-side rows.

Work the Chart, repeating the 6 rows surrounded by the thick border as described in the key and note, until Curl reaches desired size. Each row increases the stitch count by 2. Stop after completing row 12 of the Chart.

Work a final row by slipping the first stitch as if to purl and purling to the end.

FINISHING Bind off loosely using a stretchy bind off. Weave in ends. Block to shape.

Shape

Chart

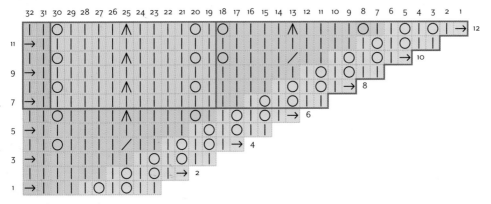

NOTE The 6 rows surrounded by the thick border are repeated to adjust the size of the Curl. The first time you work them, work the block of yellow stitches once. The second time you work them, work the block of yellow stitches 2 times. Each subsequent time you work them, work the block of yellow stitches 1 more time.

CENTERED DOUBLE KNIT DECREASE Slip 2 together at the same time as if to knit 2 together. Knit 1. Pass the slipped stitches over.

RIGHT-LEANING KNIT DECREASE Knit 2 together.

| | RS: Knit
WS: Purl

→ Slip as if to purl

╱ Right-leaning knit decrease

∧ Centered double knit decrease

○ Yarn over

☐ Repeat these 6 rows until Curl reaches desired size. With each new repeat, work the yellow stitches 1 more time.

Pretense

SHOWN IN Better Breakfast DK, a DK-weight yarn by Bare Naked Wools, in the color Daybreak.

GAUGE & SIZING Shown at 20 stitches in 4 inches in pattern as charted. The piece shown used 600 yards of yarn and has a wingspan of 52 inches.

CAST ON Cast on 8 stitches.

BODY Odd rows are wrong-side rows. Even rows are right-side rows.

Work the Chart, repeating the 8 rows surrounded by the thick border as described in the key and note, until Curl reaches desired size. Each wrong-side row increases the stitch count by 1. Each right-side row increases the stitch count by 2. Stop after completing row 12 or 16 of the Chart.

Work a final row by slipping the first stitch as if to purl and purling to the end.

FINISHING Bind off loosely using a stretchy bind off. Weave in ends. Block to shape.

Shape

Chart

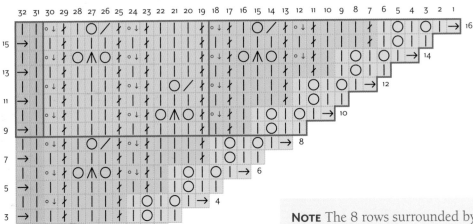

NOTE The 8 rows surrounded by the thick border are repeated to adjust the size of the Curl. The first time you work them, work the block of yellow stitches once. The second time you work them, work the block of yellow stitches 2 times. Each subsequent time you work them, work the block of yellow stitches 1 more time.

CENTERED DOUBLE KNIT DECREASE Slip 2 together at the same time as if to knit 2 together. Knit 1. Pass the slipped stitches over.

RIGHT-LEANING KNIT DECREASE Knit 2 together.

DROP AND REPLACE Drop the next stitch off the needle and let it unravel. Yarn over.

Taradiddle

16½

SHOWN IN Legacy DK, a DK-weight yarn by O-Wool, in the color Overcast.

GAUGE & SIZING Shown at 26 stitches in 4 inches in pattern as charted. The piece shown used 325 yards of yarn and has a wingspan of 50 inches.

CAST ON Cast on 9 stitches.

BODY Odd rows are right-side rows. Even rows are wrong-side rows.

Work the Chart, repeating the 12 rows surrounded by the thick border as described in the key and note, until Curl reaches desired size. Each row increases the stitch count by 1 (except row 12, which increases it by 2). Stitch counts differ on rows 14, 16, 20, 22. Do not count stitches on those rows. Stop after completing row 24 of the Chart.

Work the Finish Chart once. You'll repeat the 13 stitches surrounded by the purple border as needed to use up your stitches.

FINISHING Bind off loosely using a stretchy bind off. Weave in ends. Block to shape.

NOTE The 12 rows surrounded by the thick border are repeated to adjust the size of the Curl. The first time you work them, work the block of yellow stitches once. The second time you work them, work the block of yellow stitches 2 times. Each subsequent time you work them, work the block of yellow stitches 1 more time.

RIGHT-LEANING KNIT DECREASE Knit 2 together.

RIGHT-LEANING PURL DECREASE Purl 2 together.

Shape

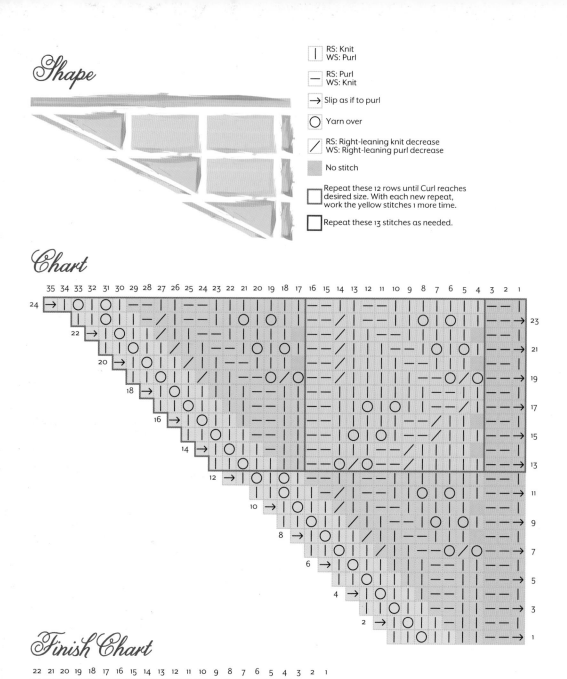

	RS: Knit
	WS: Purl

	RS: Purl
	WS: Knit

→ Slip as if to purl

○ Yarn over

/ RS: Right-leaning knit decrease
  WS: Right-leaning purl decrease

No stitch

Repeat these 12 rows until Curl reaches desired size. With each new repeat, work the yellow stitches 1 more time.

Repeat these 13 stitches as needed.

Chart

Finish Chart

Equivocation

SHOWN IN Sylvan Spirit, a DK-weight yarn by Green Mountain Spinnery, in the color Sterling.

GAUGE & SIZING Shown at 22 stitches in 4 inches in pattern as charted. The piece shown used 475 yards of yarn and has a wingspan of 48 inches.

CAST ON Cast on 8 stitches.

BODY Odd rows are right-side rows. Even rows are wrong-side rows.

Work the Chart, repeating the 10 rows surrounded by the thick border as described in the key and note, until Curl reaches desired size. Each row increases the stitch count by 2. Stop after completing row 20 of the Chart.

Work the Finish Chart once. You'll repeat the 20 stitches surrounded by the purple border as needed to use up your stitches.

FINISHING Bind off loosely using a stretchy bind off. Weave in ends. Block to shape.

NOTE The 10 rows surrounded by the thick border are repeated to adjust the size of the Curl. The first time you work them, work the block of yellow stitches once. The second time you work them, work the block of yellow stitches 2 times. Each subsequent time you work them, work the block of yellow stitches 1 more time.

3X3 CABLE LEFT Slip 3 to cable needle, hold in front, knit 3, knit 3 from cable needle.

Chart

	RS: Knit WS: Purl
	RS: Purl WS: Knit
↑	Slip as if to purl
O	Yarn over
	3 x 3 Cable left

Repeat these 10 rows until Curl reaches desired size. With each new repeat, work the yellow stitches 1 more time.

Repeat these 20 stitches as needed.

Shape

Finish Chart

Artifice

SHOWN IN Maia, a fingering-weight yarn by SpaceCadet, in the color Dark Skies.

GAUGE & SIZING Shown at 26 stitches in 4 inches in pattern as charted. The piece shown used 600 yards of yarn and has a wingspan of 60 inches.

CAST ON Cast on 7 stitches.

BODY Odd rows are right-side rows. Even rows are wrong-side rows.

Work the Chart, repeating the 10 rows surrounded by the thick border as described in the key and note, until Curl reaches desired size. Each row increases the stitch count by 1. Stop after completing row 40 of the Chart.

Work the Finish Chart once. You'll repeat the 20 stitches surrounded by the purple border as needed to use up your stitches.

FINISHING Bind off loosely using a stretchy bind off. Weave in ends. Block to shape.

NOTE The 20 rows surrounded by the thick border are repeated to adjust the size of the Curl. The first time you work them, work the block of yellow stitches once. The second time you work them, work the block of yellow stitches 2 times. Each subsequent time you work them, work the block of yellow stitches 1 more time.

RIGHT-LEANING DOUBLE KNIT DECREASE Slip 1 knitwise. Slip another knitwise. Return slipped stitches to the left needle. Insert the right needle from the right to the left into the back loops of both stitches. Knit both together. Put the resulting stitch back on the left needle. Pass the second stitch on the left needle over the first. Slip the first stitch back to the right needle.

LEFT-LEANING DOUBLE KNIT DECREASE Slip 1 knitwise. Knit 2 together. Pass slipped stitch over.

Shape

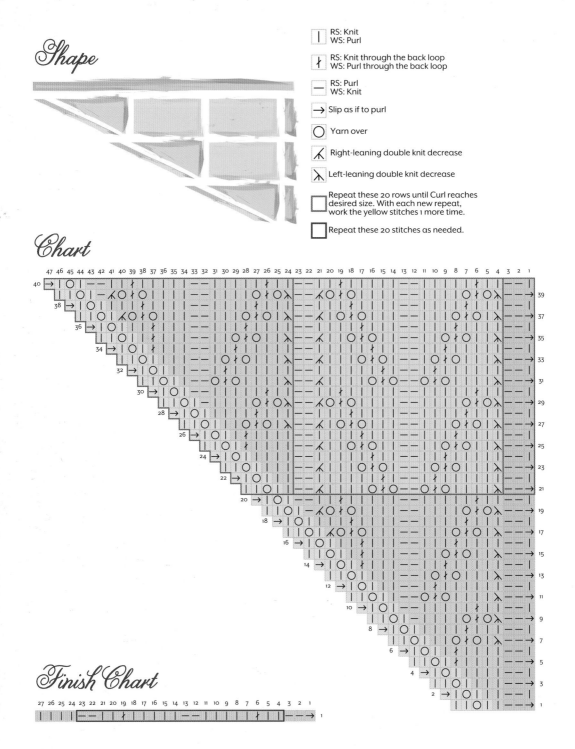

	RS: Knit WS: Purl
	RS: Knit through the back loop WS: Purl through the back loop
—	RS: Purl WS: Knit
→	Slip as if to purl
O	Yarn over
⊼	Right-leaning double knit decrease
⋋	Left-leaning double knit decrease
	Repeat these 20 rows until Curl reaches desired size. With each new repeat, work the yellow stitches 1 more time.
	Repeat these 20 stitches as needed.

Chart

Finish Chart

Cozenage

SHOWN IN Wistful, a DK-weight yarn by Briar Rose Fibers, in a custom color.

GAUGE & SIZING Shown at 16 stitches in 4 inches in pattern as charted. The piece shown used 500 yards of yarn and has a wingspan of 72 inches.

CAST ON Cast on 7 stitches.

BODY Odd rows are wrong-side rows. Even rows are right-side rows.

Work the Chart, repeating the 12 rows surrounded by the thick border as described in the key and note, until Curl reaches desired size. Each row increases the stitch count by 2. Stop after completing row 24 of the Chart.

Work a final row by slipping the first stitch as if to purl and purling to the end.

FINISHING Bind off loosely using a stretchy bind off. Weave in ends. Block to shape.

NOTE The 12 rows surrounded by the thick border are repeated to adjust the size of the Curl. The first time you work them, work the block of yellow stitches once. The second time you work them, work the block of yellow stitches 2 times. Each subsequent time you work them, work the block of yellow stitches 1 more time.

SLIP 3 Slip 3 stitches as if to purl with the yarn on the right side of the work.

KNIT GRABBING THE STRANDS BELOW Bring your right needle up under the slipped strands from 3 rows ago. Knit the next stitch. Use your left needle to pass the slipped strands over the stitch you just knit and off your needle.

Chart

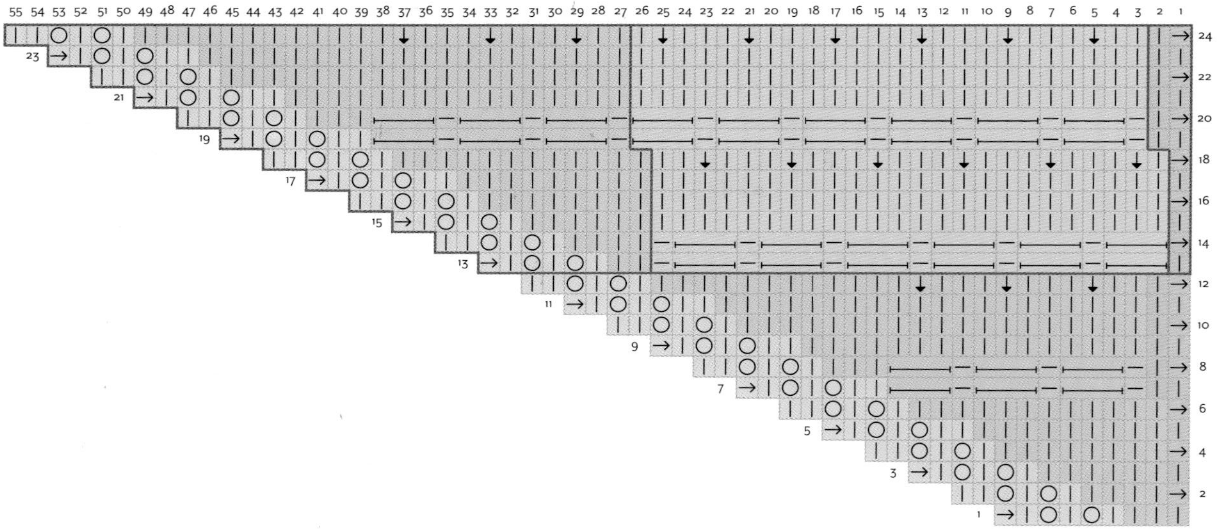

Shape

RS: Knit
WS: Purl

→ Knit grabbing the strands below

RS: Purl
WS: Knit

↑ Slip as if to purl

Slip 3

○ Yarn over

Repeat these 12 rows until Curl reaches desired size. With each new repeat, work the yellow stitches 1 more time.

Subterfuge

SHOWN IN Pure Blends Worsted, a worsted-weight yarn by Swans Island, in the color Seasmoke.

GAUGE & SIZING Shown at 20 stitches in 4 inches in pattern as charted. The piece shown used 500 yards of yarn and has a wingspan of 42 inches.

CAST ON Cast on 10 stitches.

BODY Odd rows are wrong-side rows. Even rows are right-side rows.

Work the Chart, repeating the 12 rows surrounded by the thick border as described in the key and note, until Curl reaches desired size. Each row increases the stitch count by 2. Stop after completing row 24 of the Chart.

Work the Finish Chart once. You'll repeat the 12 stitches surrounded by the purple border as needed to use up your stitches.

FINISHING Bind off loosely using a stretchy bind off. Weave in ends. Block to shape.

NOTE The 12 rows surrounded by the thick border are repeated to adjust the size of the Curl. The first time you work them, work the block of yellow stitches once. The second time you work them, work the block of yellow stitches 2 times. Each subsequent time you work them, work the block of yellow stitches 1 more time.

LEFT-LEANING TWISTED KNIT DECREASE Insert the right needle from the right to the left into the back loops of 2 stitches. Knit them together.

MAKE 1 RIGHT PURLWISE With your left needle, lift the strand of yarn between the last stitch you worked and the stitch you would normally work next from the back to the front. Purl into the loop created by the strand of yarn you just picked up.

MAKE 1 LEFT PURLWISE With your left needle, lift the strand of yarn between the last stitch you worked and the stitch you would normally work next from the front to the back. Purl into the back of the loop created by the strand of yarn you just picked up.

Chart

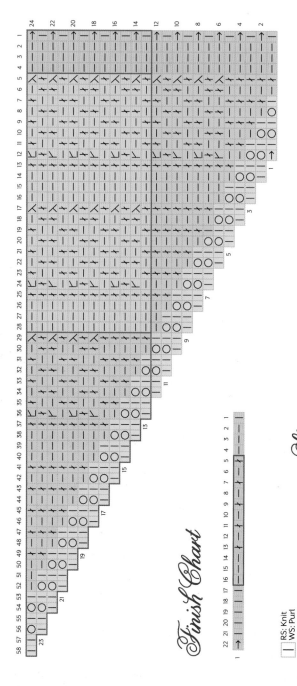

Finish Chart

Shape

| | RS: Knit |
| | WS: Purl |

| | RS: Knit through the back loop |
| | WS: Purl through the back loop |

| | RS: Purl |
| | WS: Knit |

| ↑ | Slip as if to purl |

| O | Yarn over |

| | Make 1 right purlwise |

| | Make 1 right knitwise |

| X | Left-leaning twisted knit decrease |

| | Repeat these 12 rows until Curl reaches desired size. With each new repeat, work the yellow stitches 1 more time. |

| | Repeat these 12 stitches as needed. |

Trickery

SHOWN IN Chains of Love, a DK-weight yarn by Vice, in a custom color.

GAUGE & SIZING Shown at 20 stitches in 4 inches in pattern as charted. The piece shown used 475 yards of yarn and has a wingspan of 80 inches.

CAST ON Cast on 10 stitches.

BODY Odd rows are wrong-side rows. Even rows are right-side rows.

Work the Chart, repeating the 16 rows surrounded by the thick border as described in the key and note, until Curl reaches desired size. Each wrong-side row increases the stitch count by 1. Each right-side row increases the stitch count by 2. Stop after completing row 24 or 32 of the Chart.

Work a final row by slipping the first stitch as if to purl and purling to the end.

FINISHING Bind off loosely using a stretchy bind off. Weave in ends. Block to shape.

NOTE The 16 rows surrounded by the thick border are repeated to adjust the size of the Curl. The first time you work them, work the block of yellow stitches once. The second time you work them, work the block of yellow stitches 2 times. Each subsequent time you work them, work the block of yellow stitches 1 more time.

SLIP 2 Slip 2 stitches as if to purl with the yarn on the right side of the work.

Chart

RS: Knit
WS: Purl

↑ Slip as if to purl

○ Yarn over

| Slip 2

☐ Repeat these 16 rows until Curl reaches
desired size. With each new repeat,
work the yellow stitches 1 more time.

Shape

Chicanery

SHOWN IN Marshall Island Sport, a sport-weight yarn by String Theory Hand Dyed Yarn, in the color Twilight.

GAUGE & SIZING Shown at 20 stitches in 4 inches in pattern as charted. The piece shown used 700 yards of yarn and has a wingspan of 72 inches.

CAST ON Cast on 9 stitches.

BODY Odd rows are right-side rows. Even rows are wrong-side rows.

Work the Chart, repeating the 16 rows surrounded by the thick border as described in the key and note, until Curl reaches desired size. Each right-side row increases the stitch count by 1. Each wrong-side row increases the stitch count by 2. Stitch counts differ on rows 21, 22, 29, 30. Do not count stitches on those rows. Stop after completing row 24 or 32 of the Chart.

Work a final row by slipping the first stitch as if to purl and knitting to the end.

FINISHING Bind off loosely using a stretchy bind off. Weave in ends. Block to shape.

NOTE The 16 rows surrounded by the thick border are repeated to adjust the size of the Curl. The first time you work them, work the block of yellow stitches once. The second time you work them, work the block of yellow stitches 2 times. Each subsequent time you work them, work the block of yellow stitches 1 more time.

RIGHT-LEANING KNIT DECREASE Knit 2 together.

LEFT-LEANING KNIT DECREASE Slip 1 knitwise. Slip another 1 knitwise. Return slipped stitches to the left needle. Insert the right needle from the right to the left into the back loops of both stitches. Knit both together.

LEFT-LEANING DOUBLE KNIT DECREASE Slip 1 knitwise. Knit 2 together. Pass slipped stitch over.

CENTERED DOUBLE KNIT DECREASE Slip 2 together at the same time as if to knit 2 together. Knit 1. Pass the slipped stitches over.

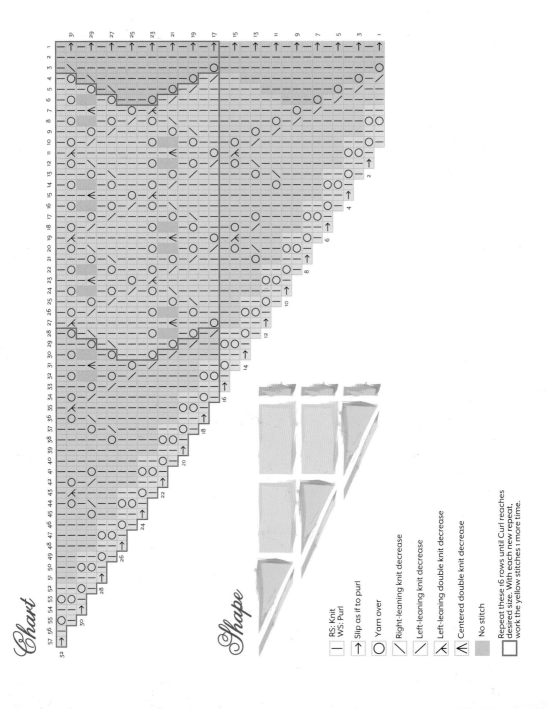

Chart

Shape

	RS: Knit
	WS: Purl
↑	Slip as if to purl
○	Yarn over
╱	Right-leaning knit decrease
╱	Left-leaning knit decrease
⋋	Left-leaning double knit decrease
⋏	Centered double knit decrease
	No stitch
☐	Repeat these 16 rows until Curl reaches desired size. With each new repeat, work the yellow stitches 1 more time.

Fakery

SHOWN IN Metalico, a sport-weight yarn by Blue Sky Alpacas, in the color Platinum.

GAUGE & SIZING Shown at 22 stitches in 4 inches in pattern as charted. The piece shown used 450 yards of yarn and has a wingspan of 48 inches.

CAST ON Cast on 9 stitches.

BODY Odd rows are wrong-side rows. Even rows are right-side rows.

Work the Chart, repeating the 16 rows surrounded by the thick border as described in the key and note, until Curl reaches desired size. Each row increases the stitch count by 2. Stop after completing row 32 of the Chart.

Work a final row by slipping the first stitch as if to purl and knitting to the end.

FINISHING Bind off loosely using a stretchy bind off. Weave in ends. Block to shape.

NOTE The 16 rows surrounded by the thick border are repeated to adjust the size of the Curl. The first time you work them, work the block of yellow stitches once. The second time you work them, work the block of yellow stitches 2 times. Each subsequent time you work them, work the block of yellow stitches 1 more time.

RIGHT-LEANING KNIT DECREASE Knit 2 together.

LEFT-LEANING KNIT DECREASE Slip 1 knitwise. Slip another 1 knitwise. Return slipped stitches to the left needle. Insert the right needle from the right to the left into the back loops of both stitches. Knit both together.

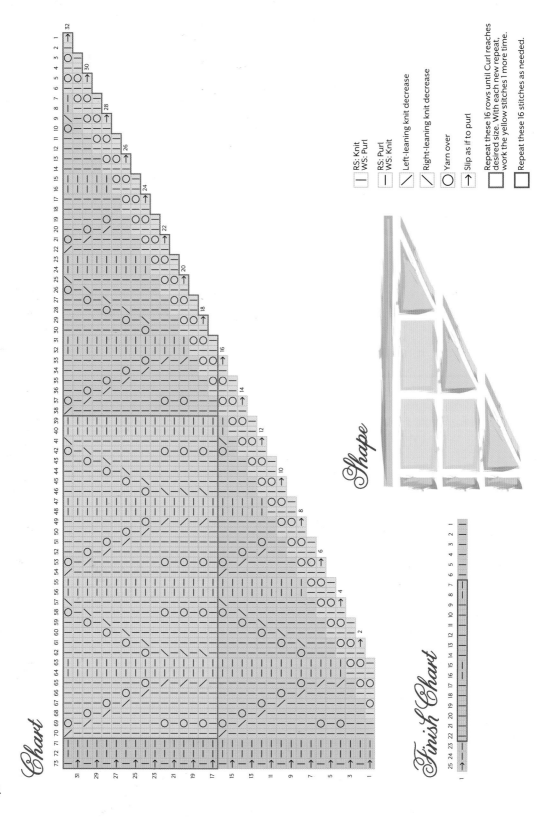

Chart

Shape

Finish Chart

| | RS: Knit |
| | WS: Purl |

| | RS: Purl |
| | WS: Knit |

| / | Left-leaning knit decrease |

| / | Right-leaning knit decrease |

| O | Yarn over |

| ↑ | Slip as if to purl |

Repeat these 16 rows until Curl reaches
desired size. With each new repeat,
work the yellow stitches 1 more time.

Repeat these 16 stitches as needed.

Thanks

I've said it before, and I'll say it again—books are a team effort. If you buy my books or knit my patterns or read my blog or hang out with me on Ravelry or somewhere else online, you're part of my team. Your support and enthusiasm keep me going, and I couldn't do this nifty thing I get to do without you. Thank you, it means more to me than you know.

My sample knitters are also a tremendously important part of my team (skilled stunt knitters every one, and totally my secret weapons). I can have ideas for patterns all day long (and I pretty much do), but without someone to turn those ideas into actual knitted things, we'd all be out of luck. Katie Metzroth, Heather Waisner, Ellen Cooper, Laura Lazarites, Heather Robinson, and Rhonda Wilson knit the pieces you see in these pages. Their work never ceases to amaze, and I am tremendously in their debt.

But beautiful knitting isn't the only thing that goes into a book. You also need instructions someone else can actually follow and writing that makes sense. Cathy Scott (she makes the amazing StitchMastery Knitting Chart Editor) and Heather Ordover (super genius behind the marvelous CraftLit podcast) make sure my patterns are clear, my charts are pretty, and I don't embarrass myself in public too often. Any mistakes that sneak through are my fault (I can't always be convinced to listen to reason), but I promise you've had a better time with this book thanks to their expertise.

And of course many thanks are owed to my friends and family. Lana Holden suffered through an endless barrage of text messages (*Which is better, this one, or this one? This one, or this one? This one, or this one? Hey what about this one?*) with astonishing grace. My dad knew just the right word when I had totally run out. And my husband, Brian, remained stoic in the face of not one but two early morning weekend photo shoots, wrote a magic knitting calculator, and has spent more time discussing the finer points of yarn and stitch patterns than any non-knitter should be expected to endure. I'm not quite sure why they all put up with me, but I'm awfully glad they do.

Sources

Feel free to substitute yarns. Just know that if you use a different weight of yarn or make your Curl a different size, you will almost certainly need a different amount of yarn.

CHARTS were created with StitchMastery Knitting Chart Editor.
STITCHMASTERY.COM

BLOCKING WIRES from Inspinknity.
INSPINKNITY.COM

MENDACITY uses about 475 yards of Rastita by Malabrigo. DK weight, 100% merino.
MALABRIGOYARN.COM

FALSITY uses about 450 yards of Devon by Black Bunny Fibers. DK weight, 70% merino, 20% alpaca, 10% silk.
BLACKBUNNYFIBERS.COM

PREVARICATION uses about 550 yards of Shanrgi La by Bijou Basin Ranch. Lace weight, 50% yak down, 50% mulberry silk.
BIJOUBASINRANCH.COM

DECEIT uses about 300 yards of Serena by Manos del Uruguay. Sport weight, 60% baby alpaca, 40% pima cotton.
FAIRMOUNTFIBERS.COM

PERFIDY uses about 450 yards of Sweater by Spud & Chloë. Worsted weight, 55% wool, 45% cotton.
SPUDANDCHLOE.COM

PRETENSE uses about 600 yards of Better Breakfast DK by Bare Naked Wools. DK weight, 65% merino, 35% alpaca.
BARENAKEDWOOLS.COM

TARADIDDLE uses about 325 yards of Legacy DK by O-Wool. DK weight, 100% merino.
O-WOOL.COM

EQUIVOCATION uses about 475 yards of Sylvan Spirit by Green Mountain Spinnery. DK weight, 50% wool, 50% tencel.
SPINNERY.COM

ARTIFICE uses about 600 yards of Maia by SpaceCadet. Fingering weight, 80% bamboo, 20% superwash merino.
SPACECADETYARN.COM

COZENAGE uses about 500 yards of Wistful by Briar Rose. DK weight, 50% alpaca, 30% merino, 20% silk.
BRIARROSEFIBERS.NET

SUBTERFUGE uses about 500 yards of Pure Blends Worsted by Swans Island. Worsted weight, 85% merino, 15% alpaca.
SWANSISLANDCOMPANY.COM

TRICKERY uses about 475 yards of Chains of Love by Vice. DK weight, 100% merino.
VICEYARNS.COM

CHICANERY uses about 700 yards of Marshall Island Sport by String Theory Hand Dyed Yarn. Sport weight, 100% merino.
STRINGTHEORYYARN.COM

FAKERY uses about 450 yards of Metalico by Blue Sky Alpacas. Sport weight, 50% alpaca, 50% silk.
BLUESKYALPACAS.COM

Other Works

So this book making thing? It turns out it's awfully addictive. It's only the first one that's hard! After that, it's ridiculously fun.

These are some of the books I've published so far. But I seem to have made something of a habit of this, so I can just about promise there will be more in the very near future.

If you want to see what's in these books, or find out what else might have shown up recently, visit PANTSVILLEPRESS.COM. And of course, if you just want to see what I'm up to, swing by VIOLENTLYDOMESTIC.COM for news of all my latest adventures.

FINE THINGS FOR PLAIN OCCASIONS: PATTERNS INSPIRED BY VINTAGE ETIQUETTE GUIDES

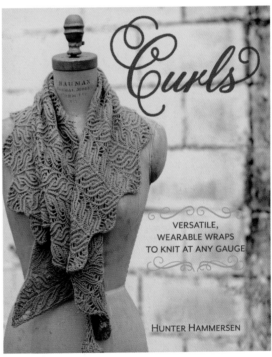

CURLS: VERSATILE, WEARABLE WRAPS TO KNIT AT ANY GAUGE